Congressional
Research
Service

Federal Reserve: Unconventional Monetary Policy Options

Marc Labonte

Coordinator of Division Research and Specialist

February 19, 2013

Congressional Research Service

7-5700

www.crs.gov

R42962

CRS Report for Congress ——————————————————

Summary

The "Great Recession" and the ensuing weak recovery have led the Federal Reserve (Fed) to reevaluate its monetary policy strategy. Since December 2008, overnight interest rates have been near zero; at this "zero bound," they cannot be lowered further to stimulate the economy. As a result, the Fed has taken unprecedented policy steps to try to fulfill its statutory mandate of maximum employment and price stability. Congress has oversight responsibilities for ensuring that the Fed's actions are consistent with its mandate.

The Fed has made large-scale asset purchases, popularly referred to as "quantitative easing" ("QE"), that have increased its balance sheet from $0.9 trillion in 2007 to $2.9 trillion at the end of 2012. Currently, the Fed is purchasing $40 billion of mortgage-backed securities (MBS) and $45 billion of Treasury securities each month; because these purchases follow on two previous rounds of purchases, they have been referred to as "quantitative easing three" or "QEIII." Unlike the previous rounds, the Fed has not announced when QEIII will end or its ultimate size. The Fed views QE as stimulating the economy primarily through lower long-term interest rates, which stimulate spending on business investment, residential investment, and consumer durables. Since QE began, Treasury yields and mortgage rates have reached their lowest levels in decades; it is less clear how much QE has affected private-borrowing rates and interest-sensitive spending. Critics fear QE's potentially inflationary effects, via growth in the monetary base. Inflation has remained low to date, but QE is unprecedented in the United States and the Fed's mooted "exit strategy" for unwinding QE is untested, so the Fed's ability to successfully maintain stable prices while unwinding QE cannot be guaranteed.

The Fed has also changed its communication policies since rates reached the zero bound. From 2011 to 2012, it announced a specific date for how long it anticipated that the federal funds rate would be at "exceptionally low levels," and over time incrementally extended that horizon by two years. In December 2012, it replaced the time horizon with an unemployment threshold—as long as inflation remained low, the Fed anticipated that the federal funds rate would be exceptionally low for at least as long as the unemployment rate was above 6.5%. The Fed argues that its new communication policies make its federal funds target more stimulative. In this view, if financial actors are confident that short-term rates will be low for an extended period of time, then long-term rates will be driven down today, thereby stimulating interest-sensitive spending. Uncertainty about economic projections hampers the Fed's ability to stick to a preannounced policy path, and any future backtracking could undermine its credibility. If unconventional policy were failing because it has undermined the Fed's credibility, the evidence would be high interest rates, high inflation expectations, or both; to date, neither has occurred.

The sluggish rate of economic recovery suggests that monetary policy alone is not powerful enough to return the economy to full employment quickly after a severe downturn and financial crisis. It also raises questions about the optimal approach to monetary policy. When is the best time to return to withdraw unconventional policies, and in what order? Should unconventional policies only be used during serious downturns, or also in periods of sluggish growth? Do unconventional policies have unintended consequences, such as causing asset bubbles or market distortions? If so, are legislative changes needed to curb the Fed's use of QE, or would that undermine the Fed's policy discretion and interfere with conventional policymaking? Or should the Fed try other proposed unconventional policy tools to provide further stimulus when inflation is low and unemployment is high?

Contents

Figures

Tables

Contacts

Introduction

In the aftermath of the financial crisis of 2007-2008, the Federal Reserve (Fed), with Ben Bernanke as its chairman, had reduced the federal funds rate to a range of 0% to 0.25% by December 2008, exhausting its conventional monetary tool.[1] With the economy still exhibiting large amounts of slack and recovery prospects weak, the Fed experimented over the next few years with unconventional policies in an attempt to revive the economy. These policies were pursued after the acute crisis phase, during which the Fed created a series of emergency liquidity facilities; a discussion of these facilities is beyond the scope of this report.[2] The dates and nature of the policy announcements are outlined in **Table 1**.

What is Conventional Monetary Policy?

Statute mandates that the Fed "promote ... maximum employment, stable prices, and moderate long-term interest rates" and that the chairman testify before Congress semi-annually on monetary policy.[3] Prior to the financial crisis, the Fed pursued its mandate primarily by setting a target for the federal funds rate, the overnight inter-bank lending rate. To keep the actual federal funds rate (determined by the supply and demand for bank reserves) near the target, the Fed regularly buys and sells Treasury securities. When the Fed wants to boost total spending in the economy, it would reduce the federal funds target. When the Fed wants to curb spending and reduce inflation, it would raise the federal funds target. For more information, see CRS Report RL30354, *Monetary Policy and the Federal Reserve: Current Policy and Conditions*, by Marc Labonte.

---

[1] All monetary policy decisions are made by the Fed's Federal Open Market Committee (FOMC), composed of the seven Fed Governors, the President of the New York Fed, and four other Fed regional bank presidents. For simplicity, this report refers to all FOMC decisions as being made by "the Fed."

[2] For more information, see CRS Report RL34427, *Financial Turmoil: Federal Reserve Policy Responses*, by Marc Labonte.

[3] Section 2A and 2B of the Federal Reserve Act as amended (12 USC 225a).

Table 1. Timeline of Major Federal Reserve "Unconventional" Policy Announcements

Date	Announcement
December 2007 to November 2008	Created various emergency liquidity facilities in response to the financial crisis.
October 6, 2008	Began paying interest on bank reserves.
November 25, 2008	Large scale asset purchases of up to $100 billion of U.S. agency debt and $500 billion of mortgage-backed securities (MBS)
December 16, 2008	Reduced federal funds rate to a range of 0% to 0.25%; anticipated "exceptionally low" federal funds rate would likely be maintained "for some time."
March 18, 2009	Large scale asset purchases which, combined with Nov. 2008 announcement, totaled $300 billion of U.S. Treasury securities, $200 billion of U.S. agency debt (later revised to $175 billion), $1.25 trillion of MBS over about one year (popularly known as "quantitative easing"); anticipated "exceptionally low" federal funds rate would likely be maintained "for an extended period."
August 10, 2010	Following completion of large scale asset purchases, maturing assets would be replaced with U.S. Treasury securities to prevent the balance sheet from shrinking.
November 3, 2010	Large scale asset purchases of $600 billion of U.S. Treasury securities over eight months (popularly known as "QEII").
August 9, 2011	Set a target date (mid-2013) for period Fed anticipated it would keep the federal funds rate at "exceptionally low levels"; the Fed subsequently moved back the target date incrementally to mid-2015.
September 21, 2011	Maturity Extension Program (popularly known as "Operation Twist"), under which Fed purchased $400 billion long-term U.S. Treasury securities, and sold an equivalent amount of short-term Treasury securities over nine months. Began rolling over existing agency debt and MBS into new agency debt and MBS (instead of U.S. Treasury securities).
January 25, 2012	Set "longer-run goal" of 2% inflation; public release of FOMC members forecast of "appropriate" federal funds target.
June 20, 2012	Extended and expanded the Maturity Extension Program to an additional $267 billion of Treasury securities, through the end of 2012.
September 13, 2012	Announced large scale asset purchases of $40 billion of Agency MBS per month for unspecified duration (popularly known as "QE3").
December 12, 2012	Announced that the Fed would continue purchasing $45 billion of Treasury securities per month after the expiration of the Maturity Extension Program; changed the threshold for ending "exceptionally low levels" of the federal funds rate from "at least through mid-2015" to "at least as long as the unemployment rate remains above 6-1/2 percent," contingent on low inflation.

Source: Various Federal Reserve press releases, at http://www.federalreserve.gov/monetarypolicy/fomccalendars.htm.

Although the policies had never been used before the crisis, they had been considered for some time. In a 2004 working paper, Ben Bernanke, then-Fed governor, and co-authors found "some grounds for optimism about the likely efficacy of non-standard policies" that central banks could use for stimulating the economy when the short-term policy interest rate (the federal funds rate, in the United States) has hit the "zero lower bound" and cannot be reduced to provide further stimulus. While the zero-bound problem had been present in Japan for some time when the paper was published, "for more than a few generations of economists [it] seemed to be a relic of the

Depression era" in the United States. The paper grouped the non-standard policies into three classes:

> (1) using communications policies to shape public expectations about the future course of interest rates; (2) increasing the size of the central bank's balance sheet, or "quantitative easing"; and (3) changing the composition of the central bank's balance sheet through, for example, the targeted purchases of long-term bonds as a means of reducing the long-term interest rate.[4]

In the aftermath of the crisis, the Fed would use all three types of policies. For communication policies, the Fed first announced in December 2008 that it would likely keep the federal funds rate "exceptionally low…for some time." This eventually evolved into a specific time horizon for how long rates would be kept "exceptionally low." In its October 2012 statement, it anticipated that the federal funds rate would be exceptionally low "at least through mid-2015." In December 2012, the Fed moved away from a time horizon for exceptionally low rates, instead tying the duration of exceptionally low rates to an economic threshold, namely as long as the unemployment rate remains above 6.5% and inflation and inflation expectations remain low, which some have called "threshold rules" or "threshold guidance." For increasing the balance sheet, the Fed has undertaken three rounds of large-scale asset purchases, popularly known as "quantitative easing" ("QE").[5] By purchasing Treasury securities, agency debt securities, and agency mortgage-backed securities (MBS), the Fed has increased the size of its balance sheet from less than $0.9 trillion in 2007 to $2.9 trillion at the end of 2012.[6] For changing the composition of the balance sheet, the Fed has undertaken the "Maturity Extension Program," under which the Fed purchased $667 billion in long-term U.S. Treasury securities, and sold an equivalent amount of short-term Treasury securities.

Since enactment of the mandate, Congress has largely deferred to the Fed on how to achieve the goals of maximum employment and stable prices, and therefore has had little input in the Fed's decisions to pursue unconventional policies. It maintains oversight responsibilities, however, and Congress has been interested in whether the Fed's unconventional policies have been consistent with its mandate.

The remainder of this report analyzes the economic effects of these programs, the current economic context in which these policies have been adopted, policy alternatives that the Fed has not pursued to date and their potential effects, potential legislative options for restricting the Fed's pursuit of unconventional monetary policy, and issues surrounding the eventual "exit strategy" from unconventional policy.

---

[4] Ben Bernanke, Vincent Reinhart, and Brian Sack, "Monetary Policy Alternatives at the Zero Bound," Federal Reserve Board of Governors, Finance and Economics Discussion Series 2004-48, 2004, p. i.

[5] Many foreign central banks have also used QE to respond to the recent financial crisis. For more information, see Qianying Chen et al, *International Spillovers of Central Bank Balance Sheet Policies*, Bank for International Settlements, BIS Papers no. 66, October 2012, available at http://www.bis.org/publ/bppdf/bispap66p.pdf.

[6] In this context, agency securities and MBS are primarily issued by Fannie Mae and Freddie Mac, with some securities issued by the Federal Home Loan Banks and Ginnie Mae. As is discussed below, the 2008 growth in the Fed's balance sheet stemmed from its emergency liquidity facilities.

Changes to the Size and Composition of the Fed's Balance Sheet

Before 2007, the Fed's balance sheet consisted overwhelmingly of Treasury securities, acquired through its normal open market operations. The balance sheet grew very modestly over time. Beginning in December 2007, the Fed undertook a series of unprecedented policy steps to change the size and composition of its balance sheet, a fundamental departure from traditional policy measures.

The Fed's balance sheet is composed of assets, liabilities, and capital; the former is equal to the sum of the latter two. The Fed's assets consist primarily of securities it has purchased, and also include loans it has made through the discount window and, during the crisis, emergency lending facilities. The Fed's three main liabilities are Federal Reserve notes, bank reserves held at the Fed, and Treasury deposits held at the Fed; these three items are counted as liabilities because they are effectively "IOUs" from the Fed to the bearer. The sum of outstanding Federal Reserve notes and bank reserves form the "monetary base," or the portion of the money supply controlled by the Fed.

When the Fed purchases assets it can finance those purchases in two ways—by increasing its liabilities or by selling other assets. In the former case, the size of the overall balance sheet increases (which has been referred to as "quantitative easing" when done on a large scale); in the latter case, the size of the overall balance sheet remains the same (which economists sometimes refer to as "sterilization"). Since the crisis, the Fed has pursued both options. Lending after 2008 and the large-scale asset purchases announced in March 2009, November 2010, and September 2012 resulted in a larger balance sheet, as seen in **Figure 1**. The Maturity Extension Program ("Operation Twist") and lending before September 2008 were sterilized, so the overall size of the balance sheet remained the same.[7]

---

[7] Increasing Treasury deposits held at the Fed through the Treasury Supplementary Financing Program was also used as a means of sterilization periodically from September 2008 to August 2011. In this case, the balance sheet was increased since Treasury deposits are a liability to the Fed, but those funds were not used in order to drain the liquidity added by a larger balance sheet.

Figure 1. Selected Assets on the Federal Reserve's Balance Sheet

August 2007 to January 2013

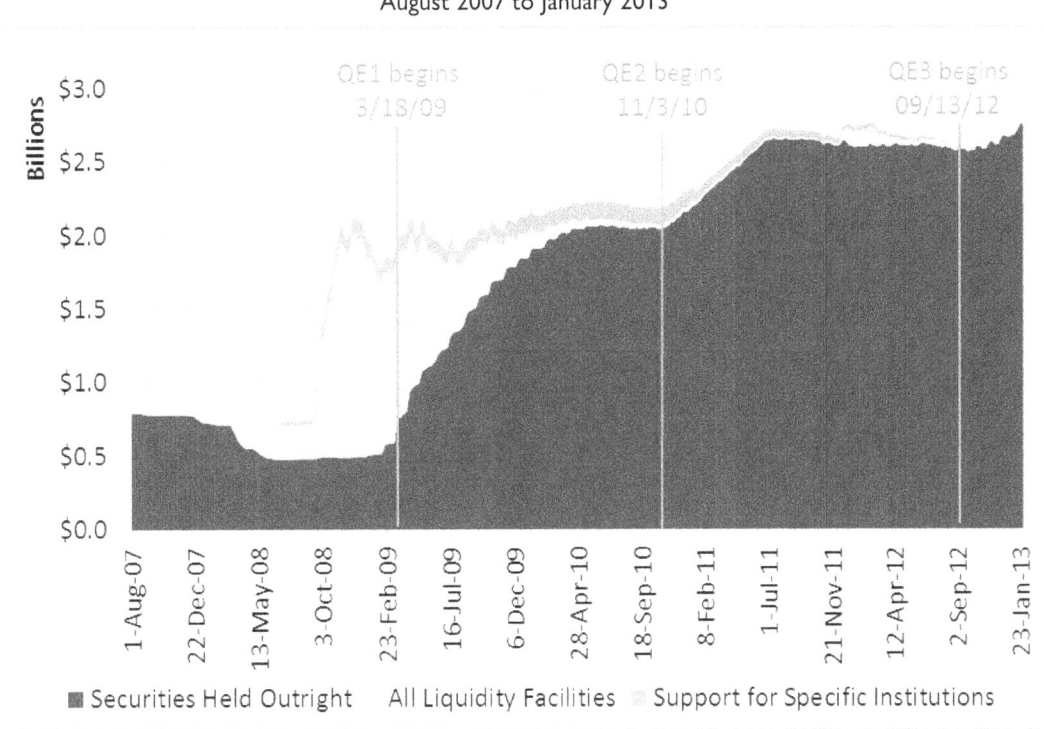

Source: Federal Reserve

Note: Securities Held Outright = Treasury securities, Agency securities, and Agency MBS; All Liquidity Facilities = Discount Window, foreign currency swaps, and widely available liquidity facilities created during the financial crisis; Support for Specific Institutions = assistance related to AIG and Bear Stearns.

When the Fed finances its asset purchases by increasing the size of the balance sheet, the primary type of liability that increases is bank reserves, as can be seen in **Figure 2**. These additional reserves, in effect, finance the Fed's asset purchases and loan programs. In the case of lending facilities, reserves increase because the loan amounts are credited to the recipient's reserve account at the Fed. In the case of asset purchases, the funds to finance the purchase are credited to the seller's reserve account at the Fed, or if the seller were not a member of the Federal Reserve System, the funds would eventually lead to an increase in a member bank's reserves when the proceeds were deposited into the banking system.

Figure 2. Selected Liabilities on the Fed's Balance Sheet

August 2007 to January 2013

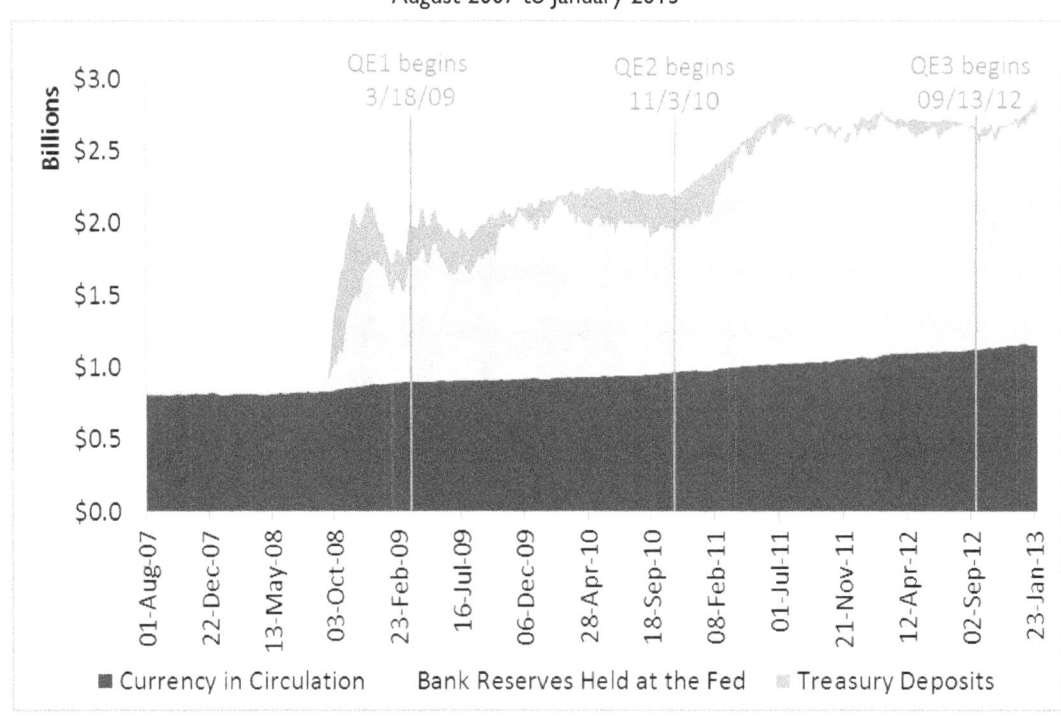

Source: Federal Reserve

The rest of this section provides more detail on the Fed's announcements, followed by analysis of the issues raised by QE.

Direct Lending and Initial Balance Sheet Growth in 2008

While the Fed has always lent to banks at its discount window, the amount of loans outstanding has typically been less than $1 billion throughout its history. Until 2008, it had not lent to any non-banks since the 1930s. From December 2007 to October 2008, the Fed introduced a series of emergency lending facilities for banks and non-bank financial firms and markets to restore liquidity to the financial system.[8] Lending under these facilities is reported as assets on the Fed's balance sheet. To prevent these facilities from leading to an expansion in the size of the Fed's overall balance sheet and the money supply, the Fed sterilized (offset) the effects of the facilities on its balance sheet until September 2008 by selling a cumulative $315 billion of its Treasury securities, as seen in **Figure 1**.

When the financial crisis dramatically worsened in September 2008, private liquidity became scarce, causing the Fed's support to the financial system to increase significantly. The increase in support made it impractical for the Fed—if it had desired—to continue sterilizing these loans through asset sales. Instead, the Fed allowed its balance sheet to grow as lending to the financial

---

[8] For more information on these facilities, see CRS Report RL34427, *Financial Turmoil: Federal Reserve Policy Responses*, by Marc Labonte.

system increased.[9] Between September and November 2008, the Fed's balance sheet more than doubled in size, increasing from less than $1 trillion to more than $2 trillion. Over the same period, support offered through liquidity facilities and for specific institutions increased from about $260 billion to $1.4 trillion.[10]

Large-scale Asset Purchases from Spring 2009 to Spring 2010 ("Quantitative Easing")

By the beginning of 2009, demand for loans from the Fed was falling as financial conditions normalized. Had the Fed done nothing to offset the fall in lending, the balance sheet would have shrunk by a commensurate amount, and the liquidity that it had added to the economy would have been withdrawn. The Fed judged that the economy, which remained in a recession at that point, still needed this stimulus. On March 18, 2009, the Fed announced a commitment to purchase $300 billion of Treasury securities, $200 billion of agency debt, and $1.25 trillion of agency mortgage-backed securities in 2009.[11] In September 2009, the Fed announced that it would complete those purchases by the first quarter of 2010. In November 2009, it announced that it would purchase only $175 billion of agency debt due to the limited availability of those securities.

Since then, the Fed's direct lending has continued to gradually decline, while the Fed's holdings of Treasury and agency securities have steadily increased, as seen in **Figure 1**. Most emergency lending facilities were allowed to expire in February 2010; by that point, emergency lending had fallen to about $200 billion overall, and consisted mostly of "legacy" loans and securities that had not yet matured. The Fed's planned purchases of Treasury securities were completed by the fall of 2009 and planned agency purchases were completed by the spring of 2010. By this point, the recession had officially ended. The net result of the Fed's actions was to keep the overall size of the balance sheet relatively constant.

Once these purchases were completed, the Fed faced a decision on what to do about its maturing assets. If the Fed did not replace securities as they matured, its balance sheet would gradually decline at a pace of about $100 billion to $200 billion per year, according to Chairman Bernanke.[12] To prevent that, the Fed announced on August 10, 2010, that it would purchase

---

[9] Chairman Bernanke referred to this development as "credit easing," rather than "quantitative easing," to distinguish it from asset purchases aimed at expanding the balance sheet. Chairman Ben Bernanke, "Speech at the Stamp Lecture," London, England, January 13, 2009.

[10] All data on direct lending and support for institutions were downloaded from http://www.federalreserve.gov/ monetarypolicy/bst_recenttrends.htm. Hereafter, these data will be referred to as "emergency lending."

[11] Federal Open Market Committee, Federal Reserve, "press release," March 18, 2009, http://www.federalreserve.gov/ newsevents/press/monetary/20090318a.htm. For these purposes, agency debt includes the debt securities of Fannie Mae, Freddie Mac, and the Federal Home Loan Banks. Agency MBS includes MBS issued by Fannie Mae, Freddie Mac, and Ginnie Mae. These totals included the $100 billion of agency debt and $500 billion of agency MBS that the Fed previously pledged to purchase in November 2008. (See Federal Reserve, press release, November 25, 2008, http://www.federalreserve.gov/newsevents/press/monetary/20081125b.htm.) Actual purchases were modest until the March 2009 announcement.

[12] Chairman Ben Bernanke, "The Federal Reserve's Balance Sheet: An Update," Speech at the Federal Reserve Board Conference on Key Developments in Monetary Policy, October 8, 2009.

Treasury securities to replace maturing securities (whether they be Treasury, agency, or mortgage-backed securities), keeping the overall balance sheet stable.[13]

Large-scale Asset Purchases from November 2010 to June 2011 ("QEII")

Dissatisfied with the slow pace of the economic expansion, the Fed announced on November 3, 2010,[14] that it would further increase the size of its balance sheet by purchasing an additional $600 billion of Treasury securities at a pace of about $75 billion per month, a process which was completed by the end of June 2011. This announcement was popularly referred to as QEII. During and after QEII, the Fed announced it would continue the practice of replacing maturing securities with Treasury security purchases. Altogether, the Fed purchased securities with maturity lengths primarily between 2½ and 10 years.[15]

Maturity Extension Program ("Operation Twist")

After the completion of QEII, the Fed took no further monetary policy actions for about six months. On September 21, 2011, dissatisfied with slow growth and continuing weakness in the labor market, the Fed announced the Maturity Extension Program, which has been popularly coined "Operation Twist" after a similar 1961 program.[16] Under this program, the Fed purchased $400 billion in long-term Treasury securities and sold an equivalent amount of short-term Treasury securities from its portfolio. The program was initially designed to end by June 2012, but nearing the termination date, the Fed extended the program to the end of 2012, which resulted in the purchase and sale of an additional $267 billion of Treasury securities.[17] Unlike "quantitative easing," the Maturity Extension Program has no effect on the size of the Fed's balance sheet, bank reserves, or the monetary base, and is constrained in size by the amount of short-term securities the Fed holds, and therefore can sell. It appears that the Fed chose this policy rather than another round of QE because most FOMC members preferred a policy that would provide some additional stimulus, but less than an equivalent amount of QE would provide.[18] By

---

[13] Federal Open Market Committee, press release, August 10, 2010, http://www.federalreserve.gov/newsevents/press/monetary/20100810a.htm.

[14] Federal Reserve, press release, November 3, 2010, http://federalreserve.gov/newsevents/press/monetary/20101103a.htm.

[15] Federal Reserve Bank of New York, "Statement Regarding Purchases of Treasury Securities," November 3, 2010, http://www.newyorkfed.org/markets/opolicy/operating_policy_101103.html.

[16] Federal Reserve, press release, September 21, 2011. The original Operation Twist was devised as a way to stimulate the economy given that monetary policy was constrained by the need to maintain the gold standard. Because such a constraint does not exist today under the current market-determined exchange rate, the Fed could have stimulated the economy through expansionary monetary policy instead, although at the zero bound, this would have been limited to unconventional forms of stimulus, such as quantitative easing.

[17] Federal Reserve, "Board of Governors of the Federal Reserve System," press release, June 20, 2012, http://www.federalreserve.gov/newsevetns/press/monetary/20120620a.htm.

[18] Federal Reserve, "Minutes of the Federal Open Market Committee," September 20-21, 2011, http://federalreserve.gov/monetarypolicy/files/fomcminutes20110921.pdf. For more information on the economic effects of Operation Twist, see the section entitled "Effect on Interest Rates and Economic Growth."

---

the end of 2012, the Fed's remaining holdings of securities with a maturity of three years or less was limited, hindering its ability to use this tool again in the future.[19]

In this announcement, the Fed also indicated that it would begin replacing maturing agency debt and MBS with new MBS, rather than replacing them with Treasury securities. The Fed's holdings of MBS, which had fallen from $1,129 billion in July 2010 to $827 billion in July 2011, stabilized at that point (agency debt holdings continued to fall).

Large Scale Asset Purchases Beginning in September 2012 ("QEIII")

On September 13, 2012, the Fed announced concern that

> without further policy accommodation, economic growth might not be strong enough to generate sustained improvement in labor market conditions..... (and) inflation over the medium term likely would run at or below its 2 percent objective.

For those reasons, it announced that it would restart large-scale asset purchases, pledging to purchase $40 billion of agency MBS per month (popularly referred to as "QEIII"). Unlike the previous two rounds of asset purchases, the Fed specified no planned end date to its purchases, instead pledging to continue purchases until labor markets improved substantially, in a context of price stability.[20]

On December 12, 2012, the Fed announced that as a result of the termination of the Maturity Extension Program, it would continue to buy $45 billion of long-term Treasury securities per month, the same rate as was purchased under the Maturity Extension Program. Unlike that program, the Fed would no longer finance the purchase of those securities through the sale of short-term securities. Instead, purchases would be financed by expanding the balance sheet, meaning that these purchases can now be considered "quantitative easing." Combined with the $40 billion of MBS purchases, these monthly purchases ($85 billion) were modestly larger than QEII. Because there is no announced end date to the purchases, it cannot be known whether this round will ultimately be larger or smaller than the previous two rounds.

Macroeconomic Effects

Economic Context

The decision to pursue unconventional policies was first made in the context of the longest and deepest recession since the Great Depression and the aftermath of the bursting of the housing bubble, which led to serious financial instability. The unemployment rate reached double digits for only the second time since the Great Depression. As measured by the consumer price index, the economy experienced deflation (falling prices) for much of 2009—the first time this had

---

[19] For the Fed's securities holdings by maturity, see http://www.newyorkfed.org/markets/soma/sysopen_accholdings.html.

[20] Federal Reserve, press release, September 13, 2012, http://www.federalreserve.gov/newsevents/press/monetary/20120913a.htm.

occurred since the 1950s. The decline in overall spending was concentrated in the interest-sensitive sectors, most notably housing. Corporations and households were reducing spending in an attempt to reduce unsustainable debt burdens following the financial crisis—a process that economists have referred to as "deleveraging." Individuals were more risk averse, seeking to store their wealth in only the safest assets, and shunning investment opportunities that would be considered attractive in normal circumstances. No matter what monetary or fiscal policies were pursued, any return to full employment in the face of these headwinds would arguably have been gradual. In the extreme case of what economists call a "liquidity trap," spending could be entirely unresponsive to monetary stimulus; this scenario is often referred to as "pushing on a string."

Since mid-2009, the economy has seen growth that is steady but insufficient to restore full employment. More than three years after the recession had ended, the unemployment rate remained above the highest level it reached in the previous two recessions. The sluggish growth rate during the economic recovery is not the typical pattern following deep recessions—usually, these recoveries feature a temporary burst of above-trend growth. Inflation has remained relatively low. The Fed chose to continue pursuing unconventional policies in light of these modestly improving conditions. Since the Fed did not pursue such policies in previous recessions, in part because it did not reach the zero lower bound on short-term interest rates, it is unknown at what point the Fed would choose to terminate its unconventional policies in this economic recovery and how willing it would be to use such policies in future recessions, which might be more typical than the recent one.

Effect on Interest Rates and Economic Growth

The Fed has stressed that large-scale asset purchases ("quantitative easing") stimulate the economy by reducing long-term interest rates.[21] Spending by households and businesses is influenced by the rates available to them, such as mortgage rates for households buying homes or corporate bond rates for larger corporations that are financing physical investment projects through bond issuance. Under QE, the Fed attempts to lower long-term Treasury and MBS yields directly through purchases that drive down their yields, in the hope that lower Treasury and MBS yields will indirectly filter through to reductions in other private long-term yields. (Lower Treasury yields do not directly stimulate economic activity—they are only stimulative if other yields fall as a result.) This could occur because Treasury securities are considered a "benchmark" against which other private securities are priced, so that other securities are automatically repriced when Treasuries are repriced (although the change is unlikely to be one-to-one). It could also occur because of a "portfolio rebalancing" effect—if the Fed pushes Treasury yields down relative to other securities, there will be a greater demand for those other securities, and investors will buy them until the yields on other securities have also fallen and relative yields have been equalized.[22] The effect of lower MBS yields on economic activity is more straightforward. Lower

---

[21] See, for example, Chairman Ben Bernanke, "Monetary Policy Since the Onset of the Crisis," speech at the Federal Reserve Bank of Kansas City Symposium, August 31, 2012, http://federalreserve.gov/newsevents/speech/bernanke20120831a.htm. During the acute phase of the crisis, QE also had the benefit of increasing overall market liquidity at a time when some financial firms could not access liquidity in private markets. This effect of QE ceased to be important once liquidity conditions normalized.

[22] The Fed has argued that the Maturity Extension Program ("Operation Twist") stimulates the economy through the same channel as QE—by reducing long-term borrowing rates throughout the economy. (See Federal Reserve, press release, September 21, 2011, http://www.federalreserve.gov/newsevents/press/monetary/20110921a.htm.) However, the Maturity Extension Program would be expected to have a smaller effect on economic growth, interest rates, and inflation than if an equivalent amount of Treasury securities were bought through quantitative easing since the (continued...)

MBS yields lead to lower mortgage rates, which stimulate housing demand and residential investment, all else equal. The pass-through from lower MBS yields to lower mortgage rates may not be one-to-one in practice, however.[23]

To evaluate whether QE has been successful in practice, it is not enough to observe whether yields rise or fall after the policy is implemented; economists need to use sophisticated statistical techniques to isolate the effects of QE on yields from the many other factors, such as economic growth and inflation, that also affect yields. Having said that, the fact that Treasury yields and mortgage rates are at their lowest levels in decades (see **Figure 3**) is strong prima facie evidence that QE has had the intended (direct) effects. How much of the decline should be attributed to QE depends on how other factors are simultaneously affecting rates. It is less clear if QE has successfully fed through to reduce other private interest rates, and thereby stimulated economic activity. The spread between corporate and Treasury bonds is still larger than it was in the years before the crisis, for example, although it has narrowed since the crisis ended. Based on "announcement effects," one study found that QEI lowered interest rates on 10-year Treasury securities, corporate bonds rated BBB, and 30-year MBS by about 1 percentage point, QEII lowered rates on the same securities about 0.14 percentage points, and Operation Twist lowered 10-year Treasury securities and corporate bonds rated BBB by less than 0.1 percentage points and MBS by 0.25 percentage points.[24] It should be noted that announcement effects measure what financial markets believe that QE will do to interest rates *ex ante*, and not what QE has done to interest rates *ex post*.

(...continued)

purchases are "sterilized" by the sale of short-term Treasury securities, potentially putting upward pressure on short-term rates and leaving the money supply unchanged. Previous experience suggests that sterilized attempts to flatten the yield curve have failed to stimulate the economy. For example, a study by Ben Bernanke (before he became Fed chairman) and other economists concluded that a similar policy in the 1960s called "Operation Twist" is "widely viewed today as having been a failure." See Ben Bernanke, Vincent Reinhart, and Brian Sack, "Monetary Policy Alternatives at the Zero Bound," Federal Reserve Board of Governors, *Finance and Economics Discussion Series 2004-48*, 2004, p. 28.

[23] For an evaluation of why mortgage rates have not fallen as much as MBS yields, see Andreas Fuster et al, "The Rising Gap Between Primary and Secondary Mortgage Rates," Federal Reserve Bank of New York working paper, November 28, 2012, available at http://www.newyorkfed.org/research/conference/2012/mortgage/primsecsprd_frbny.pdf. See also Diana Hancock and Wayne Passmore, *The Federal Reserve's Portfolio and its Effects on Mortgage Markets*, Federal Reserve, Finance and Economics Discussion Series: 2012-22, http://www.federalreserve.gov/pubs/feds/2012/201222/index.html.

[24] Michael Bauer, *Fed Asset Buying and Private Borrowing Rates*, FRBSF Economic Letter, May 21, 2012, http://www.frbsf.org/publications/economics/letter/2012/el2012-16.html. See also Joseph Gagnon, Matthew Raskin, Julie Remache, and Brian Sack, "The Financial Market Effects of the Federal Reserve's Large-Scale Asset Purchases," *International Journal of Central Banking*, March 2011 http://www.ijcb.org/journal/ijcb11q1a1.pdf; Stefania D'Amico, William English, David López-Salido, and Edward Nelson, *The Federal Reserve's Large-Scale Asset Purchase Programs: Rationale and Effects*, Finance and Economics Discussion Series, no. 2012-85, October 2012, http://federalreserve.gov/pubs/feds/2012/201285/201285abs.html; Mark Gertler and Peter Karadi , *QE 1 vs. 2 vs. 3 ... A Framework for Analyzing Large Scale Asset Purchases as a Monetary Policy Tool*, working paper, March 2012, http://www.econ.nyu.edu/user/gertlerm/gertlerkaradifrbconference2012.pdf.

Figure 3. Selected Interest Rates

2006-2013

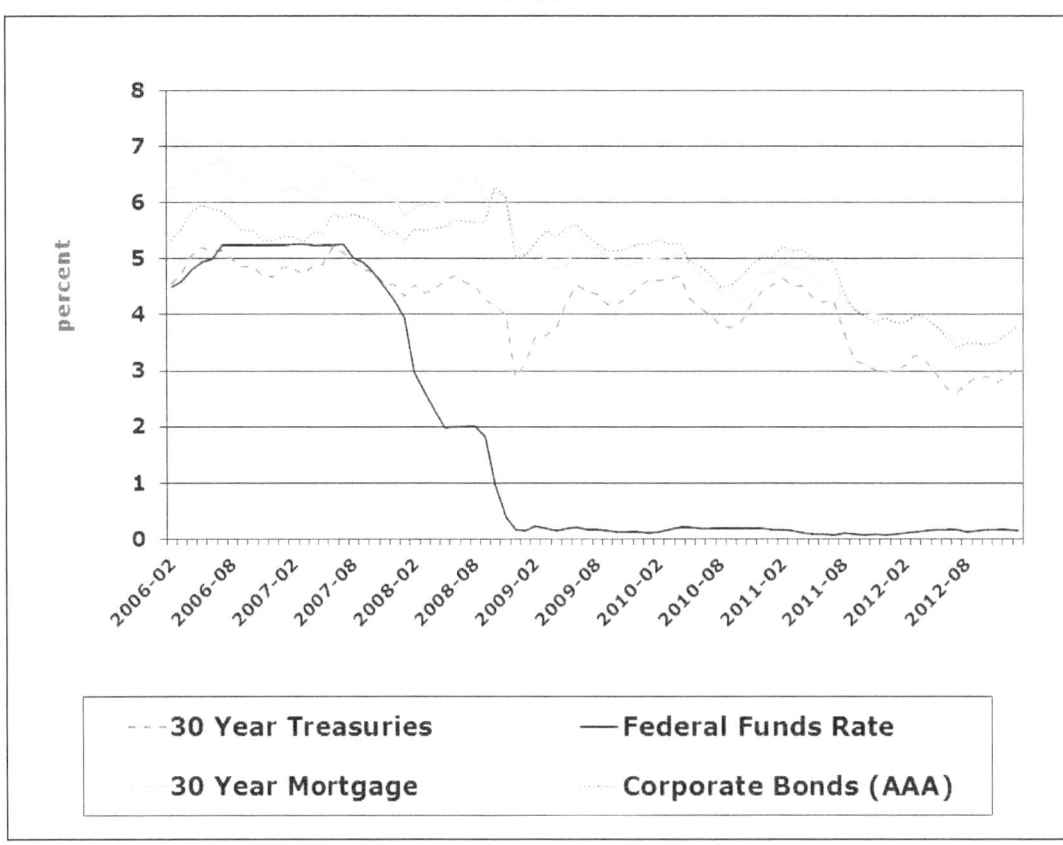

Source: Federal Reserve

Notes: Mortgage rates are for conventional mortgages.

Furthermore, if the main barrier to economic growth is not the level of rates but the unavailability of credit for some borrowers (sometimes referred to as a "credit crunch") or a desire by borrowers to deleverage, then the stimulative effect of reducing rates would be blunted. Finally, in evaluating the effectiveness of various rounds of QE, there could be diminishing returns, both in terms of how much additional asset purchases will lower interest rates and how much incrementally lower interest rates will stimulate spending. In other words, once interest rates are already very low, reducing them further may trigger relatively little additional spending.

Although the stimulative effects of QE are subject to interpretation, overall the evidence suggests that QE is not a panacea, but has had a modestly positive effect. Whether these benefits outweigh the costs depends on their effect on inflation and credit allocation and the Fed's ability to unwind QE without economic or financial disruption when economic conditions have normalized. These issues are considered in the rest of this section.

Effect on the Money Supply and Inflation

The Fed's asset purchases are financed by increasing the reserves of the banking. Banks could theoretically use these additional reserves to expand lending or other activities, which would stimulate the economy, all else equal. In practice, the increase in reserves has not led to a large increase in lending or other bank activities; it appears that banks have primarily chosen to hold those reserves at the Fed. For example, total bank lending was 5% below its pre-crisis peak in nominal terms in the third quarter of 2012.[25] Other factors besides the availability of reserves also affect a bank's decision to lend, including the cost of capital, expected default rates (which will be influenced by the economic environment), demand for loans by businesses and consumers, and so on. If available lending opportunities cannot be profitably made when all of these factors are considered, then a bank will prefer to hold additional reserves at the Fed rather than lend them out.

QE affects the money supply through bank reserves. The "monetary base" is defined by economists as currency and bank reserves and can be thought of as the portion of the money supply controlled by the Fed. Overall measures of the money supply include bank deposits and other near-money substitutes. QE leads to one-to-one increases in bank reserves and, hence, the monetary base, as seen in **Figure 4**.[26] Because banks have not used the newly created bank reserves to expand lending or other activities, there has not been a commensurate increase in overall measures of the money supply, although the money supply measures M1 and M2 grew modestly faster in 2011 and 2012.[27] Inflation expectations have not shown any lasting upward trend after each round of QE was announced.[28] Some commentators claim that QE has backfired by undermining the Fed's credibility, thereby neutralizing any stimulative effects. If this were the case, the evidence would presumably be higher interest rates, higher inflation, or higher inflation expectations. To date, none of these have occurred.

---

[25] CRS calculations based on data from FDIC, available at http://www2.fdic.gov/qbp/timeseries/BalanceSheet.xls.

[26] Unlike QE, the Maturity Extension Program ("Operation Twist") has no effect on the monetary base because there is no net increase in the Fed's securities holdings or bank reserves.

[27] In technical terms, this is referred to as a decline in the money multiplier.

[28] See Kris Dawsey, "Costs of QE Look Minor So Far," Goldman Sachs, *U.S. Economics Analyst*, no. 13/4, January 25, 2013.

Figure 4. Bank Reserves and the Money Supply

January 2008 to January 2013

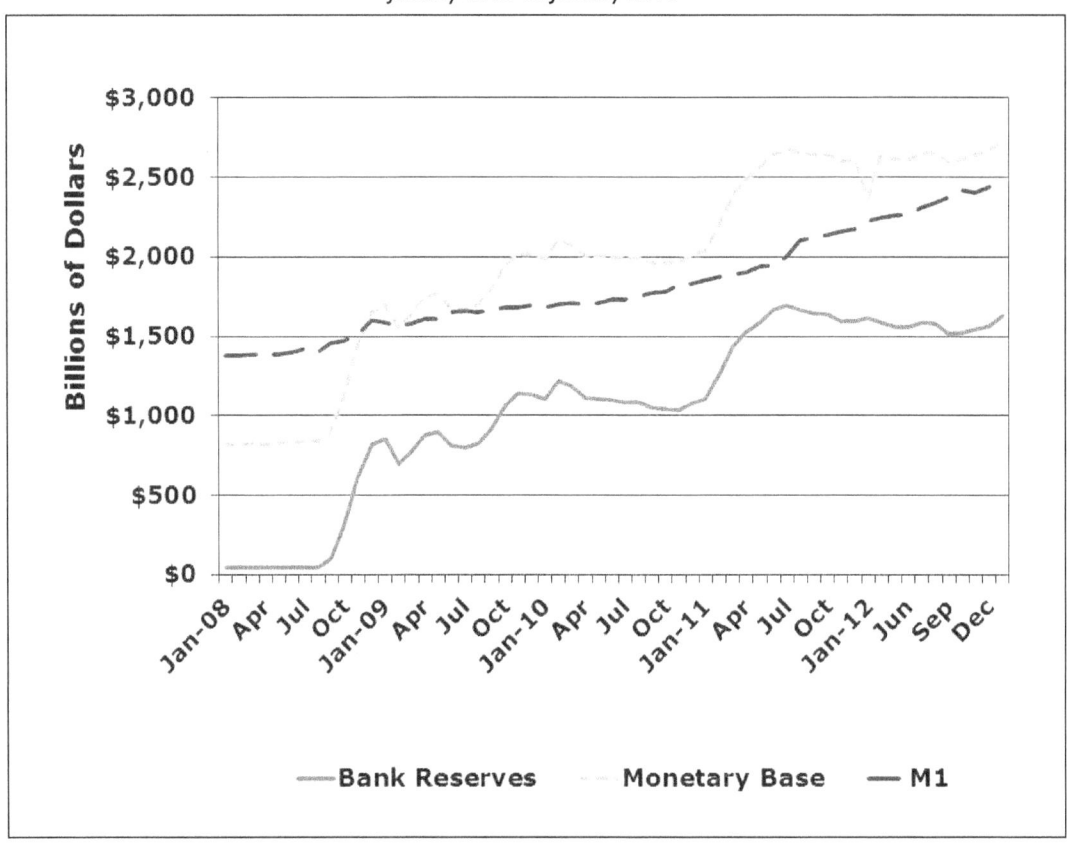

Source: Federal Reserve.

The evidence from Japan, which tried QE in 2001, suggests that QE will not inevitably lead to high inflation. If anything, the Japanese experience suggests that QE—or at least a failure to pursue QE aggressively enough—is not enough to avoid deflation (falling prices). From 1995 to 2012, Japan experienced 12 years of deflation (falling prices) and very low inflation in the other years. Although the central bank lowered overnight interest rates to low nominal levels and budget deficits were large (5.6% of GDP on average from 1993 to 2009), Japan was not able to break out of its deflationary trap.[29] The Bank of Japan eventually tried quantitative easing in 2001, but on a smaller scale than the Fed (its balance sheet increased by about 70% overall).[30] Further, some economists believe that Japan's deflationary trap was prolonged by sporadic attempts by the government to withdraw fiscal and monetary stimulus prematurely. QE was withdrawn in 2006 when inflation was still below 1% and economic growth was about 2%; prices and output began shrinking again following the 2008 financial crisis.

---

[29] On the other hand, Japan did not enter a deflationary spiral similar to the Great Depression, where deflation, declining wealth, and rising unemployment all reinforced each other and worsened over time.

[30] See Murtaza Syed et al., *Lost Decade in Translation: What Japan's Crisis Could Portend About Recovery from the Great Recession*, International Monetary Fund, Working Paper 09/282, December 2009; Hiromi Yamaoka and Murtaza Syed, *Managing the Exit: Lessons from Japan's Reversal of Unconventional Monetary Policy*, International Monetary Fund, May 2010, Working Paper 10/114, http://www.imf.org/external/pubs/ft/wp/2010/wp10114.pdf.

Although the evidence is clear that QE has not led to a significant increase in bank lending, it is worth reiterating that the Fed never intended the efficacy of QE to be evaluated by this measure. Further, even if reserves have not been lent out to date, as long as they exist, they have the potential to be lent out in the future and increase the money supply, which is an important consideration for the "exit strategy" from QE.[31]

Effect on the Value of the Dollar and the Trade Deficit

Economic theory predicts that QE would reduce the real exchange rate value of the dollar, all else equal. Assuming QE successfully reduces long-term interest rates, economic theory predicts that U.S. assets would be relatively less attractive to investors than foreign assets. Because foreigners must purchase dollars to purchase U.S. assets, a reduced net flow of foreign capital to the United States would reduce the demand for the dollar, thereby reducing its value. All else equal, a decline in the value of the dollar would increase U.S. exports and reduce U.S. imports, stimulating total domestic spending in the short run.

The real value of the dollar declined from March 2009 to October 2010, and it has remained stable since. Theory predicts relative differences in interest rates between countries affect exchange rates, and in practice, monetary policy in many countries has become more stimulative during the period of QE, potentially blunting any stimulative effects via the exchange rate (although it could still have effects through the other channels discussed above for all countries).[32] Other factors, such as changes in relative riskiness, would also affect the value of the dollar.

Impact on the Federal Budget Deficit

The Fed is a self-financing entity that yields a profit each year. That profit is largely remitted to the Treasury, where it is added to general revenues, thereby reducing the budget deficit.[33] As the Fed has increased the interest-earning assets on its balance sheet, its profits (called "net income") have increased. Net income was $91.0 billion, of which, $80.5 billion came from interest income on Treasury and agency-related securities, in 2012. Before the balance sheet grew, remittances to Treasury were never higher than $34.6 billion; they increased to $47.4 billion in 2009 and $88.9 billion in 2012.[34] Additional security purchases would be expected to increase the Fed's profits further.

---

[31] See the section below entitled "Exit Strategy."

[32] Some countries have adopted more expansionary monetary policy in step with the Fed because of their exchange rate policy, not because their economies were below full employment. Some analysts have raised fears that inappropriately stimulative monetary policy in these countries could lead to problems with overheating economies down the road. For an analysis, see Qianying Chen, Andrew Filardo, Dong He and Feng Zhu, "International Spillovers of Central Bank Balance Sheet Policies," Bank for International Settlements, *BIS Papers*, no. 66, October 2012, http://www.bis.org/publ/bppdf/bispap66p.pdf; Jeffrey Moore, Sunwoo Nam, Myeongguk Suh, and Alexander Tepper, "Estimating the Impacts of U.S. LSAPs on Emerging Market Economies' Local Currency Bond Markets," Federal Reserve Bank of New York, *Staff Reports*, no. 595, February 2013, http://www.newyorkfed.org/research/staff_reports/sr595.pdf.

[33] Other profits are paid out to stockholders (i.e., member banks) and added to the Fed's surplus as a buffer against potential losses.

[34] Data available at http://www.federalreserve.gov/newsevents/press/other/20130110a.htm.

The Fed's profits are generated by the positive spread between its interest-earning assets (securities and loans) and its liabilities. Federal Reserve notes are interest-free liabilities, and until 2008, bank reserves were also interest-free liabilities. Congress authorized the Fed to pay interest on bank reserves in the Emergency Economic Stabilization Act of 2008 (P.L. 110-343).[35] Since the Fed began paying interest on reserves in mid-October 2008, it has set the interest rate near the federal funds rate target and has paid 0.25% on reserves since December 2008. In 2011, the Fed paid $3.8 billion in interest on reserves, reducing the Fed's net income by an equal amount. Although the cost of paying interest on reserves is relatively low when interest rates are near zero, were the federal funds rate to return to a more normal level and reserves remained large—a scenario outlined in the section on "Exit Strategy"—it could significantly reduce the Fed's remittances to Treasury.[36]

Fears that the Fed's unconventional policies would lead to losses have so far proved to be unfounded. To date, the Fed has not realized any losses on its securities or lending programs and has already received more in principal repayment and interest than it paid out on all of its programs created during the financial crisis. Although the Fed's exposure to agency debt and agency MBS remain high, these assets have no default risk as long as the federal government stands behind the GSEs. Nonetheless, the Fed faces interest rate risk (i.e., higher interest rates reduce the value of existing assets) and prepayment risk on its securities. If the Fed holds these assets to maturity, no losses should ever be realized. But losses on these assets could be realized in a scenario where interest rates rose and the Fed were forced to sell them (e.g., as part of the exit strategy). One study projected that losses would eliminate Treasury remittances for a few years, but the Fed's capital buffers would be sufficient to absorb the losses, assuming the Fed's balance sheet continues to grow and then declines and interest rates (including the interest paid by the Fed on bank reserves) rose.[37] Were any losses to occur, it is unlikely that they would exceed the accumulation of higher remittances to Treasury that have occurred since 2009.

In addition to the direct effects of Fed remittances on the budget deficit, reductions in Treasury yields as a result of Fed policy reduce the federal government's debt service costs. If other spending and revenue policy does not change in response, lower debt service also reduces the budget deficit.

Is the Fed Monetizing the Federal Deficit?

Some commentators have interpreted the Fed's decision to make large-scale purchases of Treasury securities as a signal that the Fed intends to "monetize the federal deficit," which in 2009 reached its highest share of GDP since World War II, and remained at high levels through 2012. Monetizing the deficit refers to financing the budget deficit through money creation rather

---

[35] This authority was originally allowed beginning in 2011 in the Financial Services Regulatory Relief Act of 2006 (P.L. 109-351). The Emergency Economic Stabilization Act of 2008 granted immediate authority.

[36] For example, if reserves held at the Fed equaled $1 trillion and the rate paid on reserves were set at 5%, the Fed would pay $50 billion of interest on reserves over a year.

[37] See Seth Carpenter et al, *The Federal Reserve's Balance Sheet: A Primer and Projections*, Federal Reserve, Finance and Economics Discussion Series, no. 2013-01, January 2013, http://www.federalreserve.gov/pubs/feds/2013/201301/201301pap.pdf. Because the Fed does not record its securities at market value on its balance sheet, it is currently underestimating the value of these securities. Thus, the market value would have to fall below the value that the Fed is recording on its balance sheet before it would realize any losses in a sale. The study estimated that the market value of the Fed's securities exceeded the recorded value by $248 billion at the end of September 2012.

than by selling bonds to private investors. Hyperinflation in foreign countries has consistently resulted from governments' decisions to monetize large deficits.

According to this definition, the deficit has not been monetized. Section 14 of the Federal Reserve Act legally forbids the Fed from buying newly issued securities directly from the Treasury, and all Treasury securities purchased by the Fed to date have been purchased on the secondary market, from private investors.[38] In modern times, the Fed has always held Treasury securities to conduct normal open market operations. Moreover, the size of the Fed's purchases of Treasury securities was small relative to the overall deficit in recent years except in FY2011, when the federal government ran a budget deficit equal to $1.3 trillion and the Fed's Treasury holdings increased by about $800 billion of Treasury securities.

Nonetheless, the effect of the Fed's purchase of Treasury securities on the federal budget is similar to monetization whether the Fed buys the securities on the secondary market or directly from Treasury. When the Fed holds Treasury securities, Treasury must pay interest to the Fed, just as it would pay interest to a private investor. These interest payments, after expenses, become profits to the Fed. The Fed, in turn, remits about 95% of its profits to the Treasury, where they are added to general revenues. In essence, the Fed has made an interest-free loan to the Treasury, because almost all of the interest paid by Treasury to the Fed is subsequently sent back to Treasury.

The Fed could increase its profits and remittances to Treasury by printing more money to purchase more Treasury bonds (or any other asset). The Fed's profits are the incidental side effect of its open market operations in pursuit of its statutory mandate (to keep prices stable and unemployment low). If the Fed chose instead to buy assets with a goal of increasing its profits and remittances, it would be unlikely to meet its statutory mandate. The key practical difference between experiences that have been characterized as monetizing the deficit and the Fed's actions is that under the former, the goal of monetary policy becomes the financing of the government's budget deficit.

Does QE Penalize Savers?

One common criticism of QE is that it penalizes savers.[39] Just as net borrowers benefit when interest rates are lower because their debt service costs decline, net savers receive lower interest income on their investments. If this were the only factor determining the stimulative effects of QE, then less income to savers would be exactly offset by lower debt payments by borrowers, and QE would not have any stimulative effects.

There are other factors that make QE stimulative on net despite the reduction in interest income to savers, however. A decline in interest rates tends to increase asset prices, resulting in a "wealth effect" for savers who hold those assets. Overall, net borrowers are more likely to be liquidity constrained and spend more of their income (because they are younger and have lower income,

---

[38] Until 1978, the Treasury had limited authority to "draw" from the Fed to finance its deficits, and used that authority sparingly. U.S. Congress, House Committee on Banking, Finance, and Urban Affairs, Domestic Monetary Policy, *Extending the Treasury-Federal Reserve Draw Authority*, committee print, 95th Cong., 2nd sess., April 5, 1978, 26-179 (Washington: GPO, 1978).

[39] See, for example, Matthew Lynn, "QE's Biggest Problem? Destruction of Savings," *Market Watch*, October 3, 2012, http://www.marketwatch.com/story/qes-biggest-problem-destruction-of-savings-2012-10-03-81031426.

---

for example) than net savers on average. If so, net borrowers are likely to increase their spending more in response to lower interest rates than net savers are likely to lower their spending. Furthermore, inducing spending and discouraging saving are a goal, not an unintended side effect, of QE. The economic problem when the economy is far below full employment, as has been the case since the financial crisis, is that there is not enough spending in the economy to utilize the economy's productive capacity. In the extreme case, the economy can become caught in a "liquidity trap," where saving is too high and spending is too low to return to full employment even when interest rates are set at zero. To the extent that QE succeeds in stimulating spending (which is equivalent to reducing saving), the economy will move closer to full employment and total income will grow. If so, QE does not just redistribute the national income "pie" between borrowers and savers, it makes it larger. This fact illustrates that the effect of lower interest rates on borrowers and savers cannot be viewed solely in terms of the effects on debt service and interest income. For example, if QE succeeds in reducing the unemployment rate, then net savers who would otherwise be unemployed are likely to be spending more even though their interest income is lower.[40]

Does QE Distort Markets?

Conventional monetary policy attempts, to the extent possible, to have a neutral effect on the market allocation of resources. In other words, it does not benefit any particular industry or sector of the economy over others—although by the nature of monetary policy, interest-sensitive industries are inevitably more affected by monetary policy changes than other industries. One criticism of QE has been that it has had a greater effect than conventional policy on market outcomes in certain sectors, in some cases intentionally and in other cases unintentionally. QE's impact on the allocation of credit, independent of its efficacy in stimulating the overall economy, has been criticized by some economists.[41]

Through its MBS and other agency-related purchases, QE has intentionally been crafted to support the housing market.[42] The downturn in the housing market was greater than the overall decline in economic activity, and the Fed tried to stabilize that market by pushing down mortgage rates. This strategy could be criticized on the grounds that the housing downturn was a market correction that compensated for overinvestment during the housing boom; to the extent that the Fed retarded that market correction, it delayed a more efficient allocation of resources away from housing. The alternative view was that the housing downturn was an overcorrection beyond the efficient allocation of resources, and the housing market was now stuck in a vicious cycle where foreclosures and credit constraints were pushing the market below equilibrium prices and output. If this is the case, stimulus directed at the housing market can help return the housing market from its sub-optimal state to the optimal equilibrium faster.

---

[40] See Chairman Ben Bernanke, "Five Questions about the Federal Reserve and Monetary Policy," speech at the Economic Club of Indiana, October 1, 2012, http://www.federalreserve.gov/newsevents/speech/bernanke20121001a.htm.

[41] See, for example, Testimony of John Taylor, in U.S. Congress, House Committee on Financial Services, *An Exit Rule for Monetary Policy*, March 25, 2010.

[42] For example, when the Fed first announced that it would purchase MBS, it justification was that "This action is being taken to reduce the cost and increase the availability of credit for the purchase of houses, which in turn should support housing markets and foster improved conditions in financial markets more generally." See Federal Reserve, press release, November 25, 2008, http://www.federalreserve.gov/newsevents/press/monetary/20081125b.htm.

QE has also changed certain financial markets. For example, under conventional monetary policy, there was a liquid federal funds market where banks lent and borrowed reserves privately. The combination of QE, which led to banks holding large excess reserve balances, and the Fed's new policy of paying interest on reserves could cause the federal funds market to become illiquid.[43] The Fed has announced that it could purchase up to 70% of certain Treasury and mortgage-backed security issues as a result of QE, reducing the overall liquidity of those instruments for as long as those securities are held off private markets.[44] (In the case of Treasury securities, this point should not be overstated—because of the growth in the federal debt, there are still more Treasury securities held by private investors today than before QE, despite the growth in the Fed's holdings.)[45] Finally, some argue that a zero interest rate environment threatens the viability of certain financial products, such as money market mutual funds. It is uncertain whether those products and markets would be permanently compromised, once interest rates returned to a more typical range.

Another criticism is that by creating large amounts of liquidity, QE could incentivize risk taking and lead to future asset bubbles.[46] While it is difficult to judge the proper balance between risk-seeking and risk-aversion, some level of risk-taking is necessary for a healthy financial system. Because risk aversion grew intense following the financial crisis, reduced risk aversion could be viewed as a beneficial side effect of QE. Compared with the past, asset prices do not look bubbly in large U.S. markets by standard measures.[47] It is difficult to be certain, however, because standard economic theory does not provide a way to identify bubbles and asset bubbles often become apparent only after they have burst. Bubbles are undesirable because, as the recent financial crisis demonstrates, they result in a misallocation of resources and can lead to excessive volatility in the broader economy. When the output gap is deep, the economy is already in the undesirable state that a bubble might cause, so worries that QE might cause bubbles are less pressing. As the economy gets closer to full employment, the potential for QE causing bubbles becomes more concerning.

Changes to the Fed's Communication Policies

Until 1994, the Fed did not publicly disclose its federal funds target. Prior to then, changes to the target were inferred by market participants once the actual rate started changing. Beginning in 2003, the Fed began to announce in FOMC statements (in general terms) whether it was likely to raise, lower, or maintain its federal funds target in the future.[48]

---

[43] Charles Calstrom and Timothy Fuerst, "Monetary Policy in a World with Interest on Reserves," Federal Reserve Bank of Cleveland, *Economic Commentary*, June 10, 2010, http://www.clevelandfed.org/research/commentary/2010/2010-4.cfm.

[44] Federal Reserve Bank of New York, *FAQs: Purchase of Longer-Term Treasury Securities*, December 12, 2012, http://www.newyorkfed.org/markets/longertermtreas_faq.html.

[45] Goldman Sachs found evidence that QE had reduced the liquidity of certain MBS issues, but no evidence that Treasury securities were less liquid. See Kris Dawsey, "Costs of QE Look Minor So Far," Goldman Sachs, *U.S. Economics Analyst*, no. 13/4, January 25, 2013.

[46] See, for example, Andy Laperierre, "The High Cost of the Fed's Cheap Money," *Wall Street Journal*, March 5, 2012, http://www.isigrp.com/main/assets/pdfs/WSJ%20-%20Laperriere%203-5-12.pdf.

[47] For a recent analysis of potential overheating in financial markets, see Jeremy Stein, "Overheating in Credit Markets: Origins, Measurement, and Policy Responses," speech at research symposium sponsored by the Federal Reserve Bank of St. Louis, February 7, 2013, http://www.federalreserve.gov/newsevents/speech/stein20130207a.htm.

[48] William Poole, "How Predictable is Fed Policy?," *Federal Reserve Bank of St. Louis Review*, November 2005, p. (continued...)

Since 2009, the Fed has become increasingly explicit about its future plans for the federal funds target, giving markets what some economists have called "forward guidance." In March 2009, the Fed announced that exceptionally low rates would be in place for an "extended period of time." Beginning in August 2011, the Fed announced a specific time period (mid-2013) for how long it expected exceptionally low rates to remain in place. This period was pushed back a few times over the next year, most recently to "at least through mid-2015" in the October 2012 Federal Open Market Committee (FOMC) statement. Since January 2012, the Fed has publicly released FOMC members' forecasts of the "appropriate" federal funds rate target in its quarterly economic forecasts.

Beginning in December 2012, the Fed replaced its target date for exceptionally low rates with an economic event—until the unemployment rate falls to 6.5%, "as long as ... inflation between one and two years ahead is projected to be no more than a half percentage point above the Committee's 2 percent longer-run goal, and longer-term inflation expectations continue to be well anchored."[49] Some have referred to this as a threshold rule or threshold guidance. Since the Fed projects that unemployment will not fall to 6.5% until mid-2015, it does not appear that the Fed intends for this policy to extend low rates for longer than the time horizon announced in October 2012. In the September 2012 round of QE, the Fed made a similar contingent policy decision, stating that the MBS purchases would continue until labor markets improved substantially, in a context of price stability.[50]

Once monetary policy returns to normal and the federal funds rate is no longer at its lower bound, it is unclear whether the Fed will continue to announce a target date or economic phenomenon (such as a target unemployment rate) for when it expects to next change the federal funds rate. To the extent that the current communication policy is motivated by a desire to further stimulate the economy at the lower bound, as discussed below, it would arguably be unnecessary to continue once the federal funds rate target is above zero.

Economic Analysis

There could be at least two reasons for the Fed decision to announce the expected future path of the federal funds target. First, it can be seen as one change in a series of decisions during Bernanke's term as Chairman to make the Fed more transparent.[51] The Fed's current philosophy is that greater transparency makes policy more effective. In this view, more transparency leads to less confusion, and if market participants have a clear understanding of the Fed's current policy goals and direction, that policy will be more effective. Second, the Fed is trying to find ways to make policy more stimulative within the constraints of the zero bound.[52] As discussed above, economic activity is influenced by short-term and long-term interest rates. Long-term interest rates are influenced by the expected path of future short-term interest rates since a firm wishing to

---

(...continued)

660.

[49] Federal Reserve, press release, December 12, 2012.

[50] Federal Reserve, press release, September 13, 2012, http://www.federalreserve.gov/newsevents/press/monetary/20120913a.htm.

[51] For more information, see CRS Report R42079, *Federal Reserve: Oversight and Disclosure Issues*, by Marc Labonte.

[52] See the "Economic Context" section for context on why the Fed has decided to provide more stimulus during this period.

borrow for five years can take out a five year loan today or a one year loan each year for the next five years. Thus, if investors come to believe that short-term interest rates will be kept low in the future, it should make long-term interest rates lower today and interest-sensitive spending should be further stimulated, all else equal, even though today's short-term rates have not changed.

How effective is this approach? It depends on a number of factors. First, is the Fed's announced path different from what markets expected? If financial markets already expect that the federal funds rate will remain zero until, say, the unemployment rate reaches 6.5%, then the Fed's announcement would not change expectations and would therefore not reduce long-term rates and stimulate economic activity. One reason to think these announcements could change market perceptions is that interest rates had not previously been kept low for such an extended period of time in the past few decades, so market participants might have expected that the Fed would raise rates sooner based on history.

Second, is the Fed's announcement credible to market participants? If most market participants do not believe that the Fed will keep rates low for as long as the Fed has announced, then long-term rates will not decline today. Alternatively, if market participants do not believe that the Fed is committed to keeping inflation low, long-term interest rates will not fall today since investors will require a premium to protect themselves against anticipated future inflation. In that sense, an announced commitment to extended low rates could backfire if market participants believe that such a commitment makes high inflation more likely.[53]

Given the importance of credibility to effective monetary policy in general, a criticism of the Fed's new communication policies is that they could undermine credibility. This could happen if the public misunderstood the role of the central bank and its effect on the economy. Since economic conditions and projections are constantly changing for reasons beyond the Fed's control, an absolute commitment (e.g., that policy will not change until mid-2015) would no longer be appropriate if economic conditions changed after the commitment were made. For this reason, the commitment may be considered a conditional commitment (policy will not change until mid-2015 unless future projections change) rather than an absolute one. A conditional commitment is less transparent and more difficult for observers to understand, however. If it is misunderstood, credibility could be undermined and all policy decisions could become less effective. For example, the Fed moved back the end date for low interest rates several times as economic activity failed to pick up as quickly as it expected. Market participants might have concluded that the end date was changed so often that the current end date was meaningless and should be ignored. The end date could also be misinterpreted by market participants as meaning that the Fed believed that the economy would remain weak until that date, which could undermine consumer and business confidence.[54]

---

[53] Researchers at the New York Fed found that forecasters reduced their projections of the federal funds rate, GDP growth, and inflation slightly after the Fed switched its forward guidance language from "(low rates) for an extended period" to "(low rates) at least through mid-2013." The fact that the forecasters revised down their GDP growth projection suggests that the announcement may have inspired pessimism (i.e., the announcement indicated that the state of the economy was worse than they had previously believed) rather than optimism. See Richard Crump et al, "Making a Statement," Federal Reserve Bank of New York, January 2013, available at http://libertystreeteconomics.newyorkfed.org/2013/01/making-a-statement-how-did-professional-forecasters-react-to-the-august-2011-fomc-statement.html.

[54] Michael Woodford, *Methods of Policy Accommodation at the Interest-Rate Lower Bound*, working paper, August 2012, available at http://www.kansascityfed.org/publicat/sympos/2012/mw.pdf?sm=jh083112-4.

Switching from an end date to an unemployment threshold might help avoid that problem, and perhaps will require less frequent amendments to the Fed's announced policy. The downside to an unemployment threshold is that it depends on an accurate estimate of the "natural rate of unemployment," which may have changed as a result of the "Great Recession." For example, if the natural rate were now higher than the Fed believed, the 6.5% target would risk leaving stimulative policy in place too long.

Proposed Alternatives for Providing Additional Monetary Stimulus

For critics who believe that the Fed has not been aggressive enough in counteracting the "Great Recession" and believe that the unconventional policies pursued to date have been relatively ineffective, the challenge is to formulate monetary policy alternatives that would be permitted under current statute (assuming legislative changes are not pursued). A number of proposals are briefly outlined in this section. Policy options that are beyond the Fed's control, such as coupling the planned monetary stimulus with additional fiscal stimulus, are beyond the scope of this report.

Reduce the Interest Rate Paid on Bank Reserves

Since 2008, the Fed has paid banks 0.25% on bank reserves held at the Fed—equal to the current upper end of the federal funds target range. Prior to that, the Fed was not permitted to pay interest on reserves. Setting the interest on reserves at the upper end of the range raises the actual federal funds rate, making monetary policy less stimulative than it otherwise would be.[55] This policy has also been criticized on the grounds that banks should not be given an incentive to hold funds at the Fed that could be lent at a time when credit is tight. If the interest rate on bank reserves were lowered to zero,[56] banks would have more incentive to lend those funds out (or engage in other banking activities), but the additional incentive would be a marginal one. If relative rates of return were the only consideration influencing banks' willingness to lend, then there is already little disincentive offered by a 0.25% interest rate on reserves. (In practice, there are other factors at present that are likely providing a greater disincentive influencing the decision to lend.) In any case, banks could still earn close to that rate of return by lending their reserves in the federal funds market, instead of to consumers or businesses.

The issue could be viewed from a different perspective, however—what economic benefit is offered by paying interest on reserves, and does it outweigh the costs? The usual reasons offered in favor of paying interest on reserves (e.g., to put a floor under the federal funds rate, to reduce volatility in the federal funds rate, to help manage the exit strategy) are not applicable at this time,

---

[55] In theory, the actual federal funds rate should never fall below the interest rate paid on reserves because banks should always prefer holding their reserves at the Fed and receiving 0.25% to lending them to another bank for anything less than 0.25%. In practice, the actual federal funds rate has been slightly below 0.25% since December 2008, in part because some non-banks who do not receive interest from the Fed, such as the GSEs, participate in the federal funds market. See Morten Bech and Elizabeth Klee, "The Mechanics of a Graceful Exit," Federal Reserve Bank of New York, *Staff Reports*, no. 416, December 2009.

[56] In some proposals, only the interest paid on excess reserves would be reduced to zero since banks have no choice but to hold required reserves. Since most reserves are excess reserves at present, the effects of both variations on the policy would be similar.

and the interest rate on reserves could be raised whenever they become applicable in the future. If paying interest on reserves offers a marginal disincentive to lend and no appreciable economic benefit at this time, then there arguably appears to be little rationale for keeping it.

Economist Alan Blinder, former Vice-Chairman of the Fed, has proposed to first reduce the interest rate on excess reserves to zero, and if that causes no problems, to then begin charging banks a small penalty interest rate for holding excess reserves.[57] Charging a penalty rate would give banks a greater incentive to lend out reserves. However, as long as banks do not limit deposits, banks cannot directly control the inflow of new reserves they receive.[58] Furthermore, aggregate reserves of the banking system as a whole cannot fall when a bank reduces its reserves through new lending or other activities, because those dollars then become reserves at other banks.[59] (Lending out reserves would cause excess reserves to decline and required reserves to rise, however.) It could therefore be argued that charging a penalty rate on reserves would penalize banks for something that they did not cause and only indirectly influence. Further, it would create an incentive for banks to avoid accepting deposits, which could potentially reduce the stability of the banking system.

Any reduction in the interest rate on reserves would increase the Fed's net income, which is largely remitted to the Treasury, where it becomes general revenues. Therefore, it would decrease the budget deficit. It would also decrease banks' income and profits. In a competitive market, economic theory predicts that banks would pass those costs on to customers.

Direct Lending

If the belief is that the problem with QE is that it is not resulting in new economic activity, one solution would be for the Fed to lend directly, either to non-banks or to banks for longer durations.[60] Lending to non-banks could be done only under its emergency authority (Section 13(3) of the Federal Reserve Act), which contains several statutory limitations. Those limitations include that a program must be broadly based, can only be accessed when the borrower cannot access private credit, must protect the taxpayers from losses, cannot be accessed by insolvent firms, cannot "remove assets from the balance sheet of a single and specific company," and must be approved in writing by the Treasury Secretary. One statutory limitation that might make it difficult to lend to non-financial businesses is that "policies and procedures shall be designed to ensure that any emergency lending program or facility is for the purpose of providing liquidity to the financial system ... ," which might be construed as ruling out longer-term loans for the purpose of providing businesses with working capital.

---

[57] Alan Blinder, "How Bernanke Can Get Banks Lending Again," *Wall Street Journal*, July 22, 2012. In July 2012, the Danish central bank began charging a negative interest rate for bank reserves over a certain threshold. This policy was motivated mainly by concerns about capital inflows, not bank lending. The announcement is available at http://www.nationalbanken.dk/dnuk/pressroom.nsf/side/PressDNN201216563/$file/DNN201216563.pdf.

[58] From an accounting perspective, the initial result of an additional $1 of deposits is an additional $1 of reserves. If the bank subsequently decides to lend out those reserves, their reserve holdings then decline.

[59] For an explanation, see Todd Keister and James McAndrews, "Why Are Banks Holding So Many Excess Reserves," Federal Reserve Bank of New York, *Staff Reports*, no. 380, July 2009, http://www.newyorkfed.org/research/staff_reports/sr380.pdf.

[60] The Fed already makes short-term collateralized loans to banks through the discount window.

There is some precedent for such an approach. The Fed made loans to banks with a maturity of up to 84 days under the Term Auction Facility from December 2007 to March 2010. In the 1930s, under an earlier version of Section 13(3) with fewer limitations and another section of the Federal Reserve Act that has since been repealed, the Fed made a relatively small number of direct loans to non-financial firms.[61] More recently, the Fed created two programs that made credit available to non-banks without using financial firms as intermediaries—the Term Asset-Backed Securities Loan Facility (TALF) and the Commercial Paper Funding Facility (CPFF), both of which operated from 2008 to 2010. Under the CPFF, the Fed purchased the short-term paper of financial firms, non-financial firms, and pass-through entities that issue paper to finance asset-backed securitization. Under the TALF, the Fed did not lend directly to non-financial businesses; instead, it made non-recourse loans to private investors to be used for buying non-residential asset-backed securities to make more credit available to the borrowers underlying these ABS, such as consumers, students, small businesses.[62]

Another approach is underway in Britain, where the Bank of England recently introduced a "Funding for Lending" program, under which banks can exchange loans on their books for British Treasury bills for up to four years.[63] The Bank of England reasons that this will result in banks borrowing against those Treasury bills to increase their lending. This program will only work as intended if the dearth of lending is primarily driven by an inability of banks to access liquidity in private markets; if instead there are other barriers to lending, such as inadequate capital, then such a program by itself would be unlikely to boost bank lending.[64] The success of this program is also contingent on the ability of banks to earn more, adjusted for risk, by borrowing against the Treasury bills to make loans than simply holding the Treasury bills.

In the United States, the presence of over $1 trillion in excess bank reserves suggests that illiquidity is not the main factor currently holding back bank lending, so it is unclear whether a "Funding for Lending" style program could succeed here. Lending to banks would initially increase bank reserves, and as discussed above, there is little evidence to suggest that banks have used most of the increase in reserves to increase lending thus far. The drawback to direct lending to non-banks is that the Fed would have to make decisions on how to best allocate credit across different sectors of the economy. If it did so less efficiently than the private market equilibrium, it would cause economic distortions. Some would argue that if government credit allocation is merited, it is more appropriate for Congress and the President to carry it out through fiscal policy. In the case of TALF, a middle-man (private investors) was used to mitigate these concerns, although doing so raised other concerns about whether the middle-man was earning economic rents in excess of the risks borne in the transaction.

---

[61] For more information, see David Fettig, "The History of a Powerful Paragraph," Federal Reserve Bank of Minneapolis, *The Region*, June 2008.

[62] For more information on the Fed's emergency programs, see CRS Report RL34427, *Financial Turmoil: Federal Reserve Policy Responses*, by Marc Labonte.

[63] For more information, see http://www.hm-treasury.gov.uk/ukecon_fundingforlending_index.htm.

[64] Banks lacking access to liquidity could also boost their lending by borrowing from the central bank's discount window. The main reason why a program like the "Funding for Lending" program could potentially be more effective than the discount window is because of the moral stigma surrounding using the discount window to finance normal operations.

Raise the Inflation Target

Some economists have argued that the Fed should add more stimulus to the economy by modestly raising its inflation target and pledging to do whatever it takes to reach that target.[65] (Currently, the Fed has set a "longer run goal for inflation" of 2%.)[66] They argue that this would demonstrate to individuals that the Fed had a greater dedication to stimulating the economy than individuals currently believe, and a change in beliefs would in and of itself by stimulative. They also argue that it would help avoid harmful deflation (falling prices), and that the costs of modestly higher inflation have been exaggerated and the benefits have been underestimated. Proponents believe such benefits to include more flexible wages (because of the greater possibility that wages could fall in real terms while still rising in nominal terms) and the likelihood that the federal funds target will be further from the zero bound when monetary easing begins in the future, so that more easing can take place before the zero bound is reached.

There are at least two potential pitfalls to this approach. First, such a proposal seems to rest on the belief that only faster growth would lead to higher inflation, but that is not necessarily the case. Higher inflation could also occur through an increase in individuals' expectations of inflation without a change in their expectations of growth. In that case, inflation would reach the higher target, but the economy would be no closer to full employment. Second, the textbook prescription for raising inflation would be for the Fed to increase the monetary base. As a result of QE, there have been extraordinary increases in the monetary base that have not led to any demonstrable increase in inflation thus far. Unless inflation rose simply because the announcement changed expectations, it is unclear what other tools supporters of a higher inflation target intend for the Fed to use to achieve higher inflation given that increasing the monetary base has not succeeded.[67] If the Fed pledged to achieve higher inflation and then failed to achieve it, it could undermine the Fed's credibility.

Foreign Exchange Intervention

A common macroeconomic stabilization tool in small and developing economies is foreign exchange intervention—buying or selling foreign currency to influence the value of the exchange rate. Sometimes, such interventions are financed by expanding the central bank's balance sheet. In principle, the Fed could stimulate the economy by purchasing foreign currency via an expansion of the monetary base to drive down the value of the dollar, which would reduce the trade deficit by boosting spending on exports and import-competing goods, all else equal.

Standard economic theory suggests that QE would have the same effect on exchange rates and the trade deficit regardless of whether domestic assets or foreign currency are purchased. In either case, economic theory attributes the movement in the exchange rate to changes in relative interest rates.[68] In practice, foreign exchange intervention might have a "signaling effect" that makes it

---

[65] See, for example, Paul Krugman, "The Case for Higher Inflation," *New York Times*, February 13, 2010, available at http://krugman.blogs.nytimes.com/2010/02/13/the-case-for-higher-inflation/. This issue is analyzed in Olivier Blanchard et al, "Rethinking Macroeconomic Policy," International Monetary Fund, *Staff Position Note 10/03*, February 12, 2010, p. 10, available at http://www.imf.org/external/pubs/ft/spn/2010/spn1003.pdf.

[66] For more information, see CRS Report R41656, *Changing the Federal Reserve's Mandate: An Economic Analysis*, by Marc Labonte.

[67] Japan recently announced that it would conduct large-scale asset purchases until inflation reached 2%.

[68] See the section entitled "Effect on the Value of the Dollar and the Trade Deficit."

have a greater effect on the exchange rate at least temporarily, although the evidence on signaling effects is mixed.

From the perspective of the world economy, the drawback to foreign exchange intervention is that the stimulus comes from an offsetting contractionary effect (referred to as "beggar thy neighbor") on other countries, given that for any bilateral exchange rate, when the exchange rate depreciates for one country, it appreciates for the other one. Since the United States has the largest economy in the world, this consideration is likely to be important. Devaluation in one country can lead to cascading rounds of compensating devaluations in other countries that ultimately leaves no country better off (sometimes referred to as "currency wars").

Legislative Options to Prevent Quantitative Easing

Congress has given the Fed broad discretion to implement monetary policies as it sees fit to meet its statutory mandate "to promote effectively the goals of maximum employment, stable prices, and moderate long-term interest rates."[69] Although critics believe that QE is incompatible with the mandate to maintain stable prices, the Fed has argued that QE helps it meet its mandate. For example, in its announcement of QEII, the Fed stated

> To promote a stronger pace of economic recovery and to help ensure that inflation, over time, is at levels consistent with its mandate, the Committee decided today to expand its holdings of securities.... The Committee will regularly review the pace of its securities purchases and the overall size of the asset-purchase program in light of incoming information and will adjust the program as needed to best foster maximum employment and price stability.[70]

Complicating any efforts to prevent the Fed from using unconventional policy tools are two factors: (1) inflation has remained low, so unconventional policy has not proven inconsistent with the Fed's mandate thus far; and (2) limiting the Fed's broad discretion could hamper its future ability to respond to unforeseen circumstances.

Altering statute to prevent unconventional options while allowing normal open market operations would be challenging. The distinction between the two is an economic one, not a legal one. Both involve the purchase and sale of securities. Current law already limits the types of securities that the Fed may hold.[71] One approach would be to narrow the list of permissible securities. For example, Agency securities could be removed from the list to eliminate purchases of MBS and GSE debt. Alternatively, Congress could require that permissible securities other than Treasury securities be purchased only in "exigent and unusual circumstances." Narrowing this authority would not prevent the implementation of QE through purchases of Treasury securities, however.

Another approach would be to put numerical thresholds in statute that would allow conventional operations but prevent unconventional operations (e.g., set a dollar limit on the Fed's securities holdings). A potential problem with this approach is it could constrain the Fed's discretion more

---

[69] 12 USC 225a.

[70] Federal Open Market Committee, press release, November 3, 2010, http://federalreserve.gov/newsevents/press/monetary/20101103a.htm.

[71] See Section 14 of the Federal Reserve Act, available at http://federalreserve.gov/aboutthefed/section14.htm.

than intended, particularly since the Fed's securities holdings gradually increase under conventional policy. This points to the underlying tension between the desire for the Fed to have broad discretion to rapidly react to unforeseen circumstances and the potential for the Fed to use that discretion in such a way that meets the disapproval of some or all Members of Congress.

Analysis of more fundamental changes to the Federal Reserve's powers, such as a return to the gold standard, that would affect its ability to conduct QE are beyond the scope of this report.

Exit Strategy

Quantitative easing has the potential to lead to high inflation if banks decided to begin using their reserve holdings to rapidly increase their lending, which would lead to a rapid increase in the money supply. In that case, the Fed would need an "exit strategy" from QE that could be implemented relatively quickly.[72] The most straightforward method would be for the Fed to withdraw those reserves from the banking system by selling some of its assets and not replacing assets as they mature. This would reduce the size of its balance sheet on both the assets and liabilities side. It is uncertain how many assets would need to be sold, but to give an order of magnitude, the balance sheet is more than three times larger than it was before the crisis. By April 2010, the Fed's balance sheet consisted predominantly of securities that could be sold in secondary markets. These can mostly be sold relatively quickly in theory, although there could be political resistance in practice. Given the Fed's concerns about the fragility of housing markets, it is not clear how its mortgage-related holdings could be reduced quickly if the Fed became concerned about rising inflation. Selling only Treasury securities might not reduce the balance sheet sufficiently, given the amount of Treasury securities the Fed might feel comfortable selling. The furthest that the Fed has reduced its Treasury holdings in the past was to approximately $480 billion in 2008.

Another option would be to give banks incentives not to lend out reserves by raising the interest rate that the Fed pays on reserves, thereby keeping the larger monetary base from increasing the broader money supply.[73] Since there is no domestic and very little international experience with first increasing the base and then tightening policy without reversing the increase in the monetary base, this strategy can be considered untested.[74] To better prevent these reserves from

---

[72] The Fed's views on the issues outlined in this section can be read in Ben Bernanke, "The Fed's Exit Strategy," *Wall Street Journal*, July 21, 2009, p. A15. See also Claudio Borio and Piti Disyatat, *Unconventional Monetary Policies: An Appraisal*," Bank for International Settlements, Working Paper 292, November 2009; John Taylor, "An Exit Rule for Monetary Policy," Testimony before the Committee on Financial Services, U.S. House of Representatives, March 25, 2010.

[73] Economist Alan Blinder argues that the interest on reserves can help ensure that an exit strategy of selling assets is not disruptive. Alan Blinder, "Quantitative Easing: Entrance and Exit Strategies," *Federal Reserve Bank of St. Louis Review*, vol. 92, no. 6, November 2010, p. 465.

[74] One paper looks at international experience with paying interest on bank reserves to answer this question. There is very limited experience with raising short-term interest rates while maintaining excess reserve balances, however. Japan in the 1990s is the best-known case of quantitative easing, and it removed excess reserves before raising rates. The authors found that Norway had successfully raised rates while maintaining excess reserves from 2005 to 2008, although they did reduce reserves by half during that period. David Bowman, Etienne Gagnon, Mike Leahy, "Interest on Excess Reserves as a Monetary Policy Instrument: The Experience of Foreign Central Banks," Federal Reserve Board, *International Finance Discussion Paper 996*, March 2010. See also Richard Anderson et al., "Doubling Your Monetary Base and Surviving: Some International Experience," *Federal Reserve Bank of St. Louis Review*, vol. 92, no. 6, November 2010, p. 481.

being lent out if necessary, the Fed began offering "term deposits" with a one- to six-month maturity for bank reserves in 2010. The interest rate on these term deposits is set through auction; banks would presumably be willing to bid for term deposits only if the interest rate exceeded the rate paid by the Fed on normal reserves.

The Fed could also attempt to reduce liquidity by lending its assets out through "reverse repos."[75] This would change the composition of liabilities on the Fed's balance sheet, replacing its other liabilities with reverse repos. It is unlikely that reverse repos operations could be large enough to remove most of the new liquidity, however.[76]

Treasury cash balances held at the Fed could also be used to tie up excess liquidity if needed. The Treasury announced the Supplementary Financing Program on September 17, 2008, as an alternative method for the Fed to increase its assistance to the financial sector without increasing the amount of money in circulation.[77] Under this program, the Treasury has temporarily auctioned more new securities than it needs to finance government operations and has deposited the proceeds at the Fed. (The operations do not affect inflation because the money received by the Treasury is held at the Fed and not allowed to circulate in the economy.) Since August 2011, the balance in the Supplementary Financing Program has been zero. Given that the size of this program is constrained by the debt limit, it would be insufficient to significantly reduce liquidity without a large increase in the debt limit.[78]

When the time comes, the Fed might decide to employ one or some combination of these tools to implement the exit strategy. There has been some discussion of the proper sequencing of events, and whether the use of conventional and unconventional policy tools might overlap. For example, Chairman Bernanke has stated that he anticipates that the Fed will not sell securities until policy tightening is already under way.[79] In this scenario, raising the interest rate on reserves would presumably be crucial to the exit strategy, since the current size of the balance sheet (and accompanying level of bank reserves) is otherwise inconsistent with a higher federal funds rate.

It is unclear whether there is any economic benefit to pursuing an exit strategy that maintains a large balance sheet. Any stimulative effect of a larger balance sheet on the economy would be offset by the effects of paying interest on reserves, reverse repos, the Treasury Supplementary Program, or issuing Fed bonds. The large balance sheet would have no positive effect on aggregate demand if it is offset by any of these actions that drain liquidity from the economy. If

---

[75] A reverse repo (or reverse repurchase agreement) is a purchase of securities with an agreement to resell them at a higher price at a specific future date. The transaction is economically equivalent to a loan, with the securities serving as collateral.

[76] The size of reverse repo operations is limited to the amount of securities held by the Fed available to lend and private investors' willingness to borrow them. In recent years, the Fed's reverse repos outstanding have not exceeded $108 billion. Goldman Sachs reports that Fed officials have indicated that they do not believe private investors could absorb more than $100 billion in reverse repos. Ed McKelvey, "Fed Lays Groundwork to Offset Another Increase in Excess Reserves," *U.S. Daily Newsletter*, September 24, 2009.

[77] The Treasuries issued under the program are indistinguishable to investors from regularly-issued securities.

[78] The Fed and Treasury announced in March 2009 that they would seek "legislative action to provide additional tools the Federal Reserve can use to sterilize the effects of its lending or securities purchases on the supply of bank reserves." Many analysts interpreted this statement to express the desire for the Fed to gain authority to issue its own bonds. To date, legislation to allow the Fed to do so has not been considered, and the idea has not been widely discussed since.

[79] Testimony of Fed Chairman Ben Bernanke, in U.S. Congress, House Committee on Financial Services, *Federal Reserve's Exit Strategy*, February 10, 2010, http://www.federalreserve.gov/newsevents/testimony/bernanke20100210a.htm.

---

investors have rational expectations, it is not clear how this strategy could flatten the yield curve either, because the long end of the yield curve is determined primarily by expectations of future interest rates, and sterilized purchases of assets in the present should not change those expectations, all else equal. After the federal funds rate has been raised from the zero bound, it remains to be seen whether the Fed would continue using balance sheet operations or would prefer to eventually return to using only conventional monetary policy tools.

To date, quantitative easing has not had any noticeable effect on the public's inflationary expectations.[80] If inflationary expectations remain low, it would be expected to make an exit strategy, and monetary policy generally, more effective. On the other hand, one criticism of QE is that it could at some point undermine expectations of low and stable inflation, and the Fed's credibility on inflation. If inflationary expectations rise, larger-scale operations than would otherwise be needed could become necessary for an exit strategy. In a worst case scenario, a rise in inflationary expectations could force the Fed to pursue an exit strategy before the economy has recovered, thereby risking "stagflation" (stagnant growth with high inflation).

Concluding Thoughts

The Fed initially undertook its unconventional policies in 2009 in response to the deepest and longest recession since the Great Depression. At the time, financial stability was still fragile, unemployment was in double digits, and inflation was very low, with fears among some economists that deflation would emerge. Since the second half of 2009, the economy has expanded at a steady but slow pace that has gradually reduced unemployment but has not yet returned the economy to full employment. Over the same period, inflation has continued to remain low and inflation expectations have remained relatively steady. An individual's view on whether the Fed's unconventional policies are currently justified, or whether the Fed should be undertaking more or less stimulus than it has, depends in large part on whether one believes that the Fed should do more or less in the face of slow but steady economic expansion. Some might feel comfortable with unconventional policy during periods of economic free fall, such as late 2008, but feel uncomfortable with unconventional policy once the economy has stabilized.

Although it is difficult to disentangle the effects of the Fed's policies from other factors affecting interest rates, the fact that Treasury and MBS yields are at their lowest levels in decades suggests that the Fed's unconventional policies have had the direct effects that were intended. It is less clear to what extent lower Treasury and MBS yields have fed through to lower private interest rates, a greater supply of private credit, and more interest-sensitive spending. Corporate and household deleveraging and risk aversion following the crisis has driven interest-sensitive spending down, so lower rates can only accomplish so much in the face of these headwinds. It is clear at this point that monetary policy alone is not potent enough to return the economy to full employment quickly, and there may be diminishing economic benefits from additional QE. Given that it is unlikely that the economy would return to full employment significantly sooner if the Fed purchased assets at a faster pace, some have argued for policies that are even more unconventional as a means to additional monetary stimulus. The economic benefits of such policies would need to be weighed against their costs—the economic risk that they would lead to

---

[80] By standard measures, inflation expectations have fluctuated around relatively low levels in the last decade, with one exception: they dropped near zero during the financial crisis, and have since returned to pre-crisis levels.

high inflation and the political risk that they would undermine the Fed's political support and possibly its credibility.

While the economic benefits of unconventional policy (monetary stimulus) have not been sufficient to restore full employment, the main perceived risks (higher inflation or higher inflationary expectations) have not yet materialized several years after QE began. Thus, while some might argue that there has been limited upside from these policies, it could be argued that there has been limited downside to date. Some critics fear that unconventional policy is undermining the Fed's credibility, and this could harm the future effectiveness of monetary policy. If unconventional policy were failing because it is undermining the Fed's credibility, the evidence would be high interest rates, high inflation expectations, or both; to date, neither has occurred. At this point, the main drawback to unconventional policy is a hypothetical one: that it may complicate a smooth transition to conventional monetary policy when the economy has returned to normal, particularly because the "exit strategy" is untested.

Author Contact Information

Marc Labonte

Coordinator of Division Research and Specialist
mlabonte@crs.loc.gov, 7-0640